THE EVOLUTION OF DISTANCE LEARNING

FROM CORRESPONDENCE COURSES TO ONLINE EDUCATION

DR. SRI RAGHAVA

For all the educators and learners who embrace the transformative power of online education, and for those who continue to push the boundaries of knowledge in the digital age.

Contents

Preface   *vii*

  1. Introduction To Distance And Online Education   1

  2. Foundations Of Online Learning   13

  3. Technology In Online Education   22

  4. Designing Online Courses   30

  5. Teaching Strategies For Online Environments   38

  6. Student Support And Success In Online Learning   45

  7. Assessment And Evaluation In Online Education   57

  8. Professional Development For Online Educators   65

  9. Policy And Institutional Considerations   77

10. Future Trends And Innovations   87

11. Conclusion   96

PREFACE

Welcome to the world of distance and online education! In today's rapidly evolving landscape of education, the advent of digital technologies has brought about transformative changes in how we teach and learn. This book serves as a comprehensive guide to understanding the concepts, evolution, challenges, and opportunities within the realm of distance and online education.

As educators, administrators, policymakers, and learners alike navigate the complexities of online learning, it becomes increasingly important to explore the fundamental principles and practices that underpin this mode of education. This book aims to provide readers with a deep dive into the multifaceted aspects of distance and online education, offering insights, strategies, and best practices for success in virtual learning environments.

The journey begins with an exploration of the definition and historical evolution of distance education, tracing its roots from early correspondence courses to the digital age of online learning. We delve into key concepts, pedagogical theories, and technological advancements shaping the field, offering practical guidance on designing engaging and effective online courses.

Throughout the book, we examine the challenges and opportunities inherent in online education, from ensuring accessibility and inclusivity to maintaining academic integrity and quality assurance. We also explore emerging trends, innovations, and future directions in distance and online learning, envisioning a future where education knows no boundaries.

This book is intended for educators seeking to enhance their online teaching practices, administrators tasked with leading online education initiatives, policymakers shaping the future of digital learning, and learners navigating the virtual classroom. Whether you are new to online education or a seasoned veteran, there is something for everyone in these pages.

As we embark on this journey together, let us embrace the transformative power of distance and online education to empower learners, foster innovation, and create a more equitable and inclusive world. Thank you for joining us on this adventure into the exciting realm of virtual learning.

Warm regards,

Dr. Sri Raghava

I

Introduction to Distance and Online Education

In the world of education, something big has changed: distance and online learning. These let people learn without being in a physical classroom. In this introduction, we'll explore what distance and online learning are all about and why it's important to know their history.

Understanding the Ideas

Distance learning started with sending lessons by mail and grew to help people learn from far away. Online learning took it further, using the internet to connect people and share knowledge.

Why It Matters

It's important to understand where distance and online learning came from because it helps us see where they're going. By looking back at the challenges and achievements, we can better understand how education is changing and where it might go next.

Joining the Journey

As we start this journey, let's explore how education has evolved over time and how technology is shaping its future. With every step, we'll discover new ideas and possibilities in the world of distance and online learning.

Defining Distance Education

Distance education is a way of teaching and learning that doesn't require students to be in a regular classroom. Instead, it reaches them wherever they are, using various methods like mail, email, video, or online platforms.

Historical Origins

Distance education isn't new. It began long ago with things like sending lessons by mail or radio. One early example is "correspondence courses," where students would get lessons and send back their work. Over time, technology made distance learning easier, leading to the online education we have today.

Top of Form

Evolution of Distance Education

Distance education has undergone a remarkable evolution, propelled by key milestones, visionary leaders, and technological innovations that have transformed the way we teach and learn beyond the confines of traditional classrooms.

Early Beginnings

Distance education traces its origins back centuries, with early examples including correspondence courses exchanged via mail. One notable milestone occurred in the 19th century when the Industrial Revolution spurred the growth of correspondence education, enabling individuals to access learning materials from afar.

Pioneers and Institutions

Throughout history, pioneers and institutions have played pivotal roles in advancing distance education. One such figure is Isaac Pitman, who developed shorthand writing and introduced correspondence courses in the 19th century. Similarly, the University of London became a trailblazer in distance education with the establishment of its External Programme in 1858, offering degrees to students worldwide.

Technological Innovations

The evolution of distance education accelerated with the advent of new technologies. The introduction of radio and television in the 20th century enabled the broadcast of educational programs to remote audiences, expanding access to learning. However, it was the digital revolution of the late 20th and early 21st centuries that truly revolutionized distance education. The emergence of computers, the internet, and multimedia technologies paved the way for online learning platforms, interactive courseware, and virtual classrooms, transforming distance education into online education as we know it today.

Global Expansion

As distance education evolved, it transcended geographical boundaries, offering educational opportunities to learners worldwide. Institutions like the Open University in the United Kingdom and the Indira Gandhi National Open University in India became pioneers in providing distance education on a massive scale, reaching millions of students across continents.

Current Trends and Future Prospects

Today, distance education continues to evolve, driven by emerging technologies, changing pedagogical approaches, and the increasing demand for flexible learning options. Massive Open Online Courses (MOOCs), mobile learning, and artificial intelligence are reshaping the landscape of distance education, offering new possibilities for personalized, adaptive learning experiences.

In the realm of distance and online education, understanding key concepts and terminology is essential for navigating the diverse landscape of learning environments. Below are explanations of some commonly used terms:

1. **Asynchronous Learning**:

   - Asynchronous learning refers to a type of learning where students engage with course materials and complete activities at different times, rather than in real-time. This allows for flexibility in scheduling and accommodates learners with varying schedules and time zones.

2. **Synchronous Learning**:

   - Synchronous learning involves real-time interaction between instructors and students, typically facilitated through live lectures, webinars, or virtual classrooms. Participants engage in discussions, ask questions, and receive immediate feedback, simulating a traditional classroom experience.

3. **Blended Learning**:

   - Blended learning, also known as hybrid learning, combines face-to-face instruction with online learning components. It integrates traditional classroom activities with digital tools and resources, offering flexibility and personalized learning experiences. Blended learning models vary widely, with some courses featuring equal parts online and in-person instruction, while others blend the two formats seamlessly throughout the curriculum.

4. **Virtual Learning Environment (VLE)**:

  - A virtual learning environment, sometimes referred to as a learning management system (LMS) or course management system (CMS), is an online platform used to deliver educational content, facilitate communication between instructors and students, and manage learning activities. VLEs typically include features such as course materials, discussion forums, assignment submission tools, and grading functionalities.

5. **MOOC (Massive Open Online Course)**:

  - MOOCs are online courses designed to accommodate large numbers of participants simultaneously. They are typically open to anyone with internet access and are often offered free of charge. MOOCs cover a wide range of subjects and are characterized by their scalability, interactivity, and accessibility.

6. **Flipped Classroom**:

  - In a flipped classroom model, traditional teaching methods are inverted, with students accessing instructional content online outside of class and engaging in active learning activities, discussions, or projects during class time. This approach allows for more personalized instruction, promotes student engagement, and fosters deeper learning experiences.

The Digital Revolution and Its Impact

The advent of the digital revolution has ushered in a new era in education, fundamentally transforming the way knowledge is created, disseminated, and accessed. This section explores the profound impact of the digital revolution on the educational landscape, with a focus on how online education has democratized access to learning and expanded educational opportunities globally.

1. Access to Information and Resources

The digital revolution has democratized access to information and resources, breaking down barriers to learning that were once insurmountable. With a wealth of educational content available online, learners from diverse backgrounds and geographical locations can access high-quality materials on virtually any subject, empowering them to pursue their educational goals independently.

2. Flexibility and Convenience

Online education offers unprecedented flexibility and convenience, allowing learners to engage with course materials and participate in learning activities at their own pace and on their own schedule. Whether juggling work and family responsibilities or residing in remote areas with limited access to traditional educational institutions, students can now pursue their studies from anywhere in the world with an internet connection.

3. Customized Learning Experiences

The digital revolution has enabled the development of personalized and adaptive learning technologies, tailoring educational experiences to the individual needs and preferences of learners. Through data-driven insights and analytics, online platforms can track student progress, identify areas for improvement, and deliver targeted interventions to enhance learning outcomes, fostering a more dynamic and responsive educational environment.

4. Global Collaboration and Networking

Online education has facilitated unprecedented opportunities for global collaboration and networking, connecting learners and educators from diverse cultural backgrounds and geographical locations. Through virtual classrooms, online discussion forums, and collaborative projects, students can engage in cross-cultural exchanges, share perspectives, and collaborate on projects that transcend borders, enriching their educational experience and expanding their worldview.

5. Lifelong Learning and Professional Development

The digital revolution has democratized access to lifelong learning and professional development opportunities, enabling individuals to acquire new skills, advance their careers, and pursue their passions throughout their lives. With a wealth of online courses, certifications, and micro-credentials available, learners can continuously upskill and reskill to meet the evolving demands of the global economy and stay competitive in their chosen fields.

Challenges and Opportunities in Distance and Online Education

Distance and online education have revolutionized the way we learn, offering unprecedented opportunities for access and flexibility. However, they also present unique challenges that must be addressed to ensure equitable access, maintain high quality, and maximize the potential benefits of digital learning. This section examines both the challenges and opportunities inherent in distance and online education.

1. Challenges

a. Equity and Access:

- Despite the promise of online education to democratize access to learning, digital inequality remains a significant barrier for many learners. Disparities in access to technology, reliable internet connectivity, and digital literacy skills disproportionately affect marginalized communities, exacerbating existing inequities in education.
- Rural areas and underserved populations often lack the infrastructure and resources necessary to fully participate in online learning, limiting their access to educational opportunities and perpetuating socio-economic disparities.

b. Quality Assurance:

- Ensuring the quality of online education programs and courses poses a considerable challenge for institutions and educators. Maintaining rigorous academic standards, fostering meaningful engagement, and assessing learning outcomes in digital environments require innovative pedagogical approaches and robust quality assurance mechanisms.
- Addressing concerns related to academic integrity, plagiarism, and cheating in online assessments is another ongoing challenge, requiring proactive measures to safeguard the integrity and credibility of online credentials.

c. Student Engagement and Motivation:

- Online learning environments can sometimes lack the social interaction and immediacy of face-to-face instruction, posing challenges for student engagement and motivation. Without the structure and accountability of traditional classrooms, students may struggle to stay focused, participate actively, and persist in their studies.
- Overcoming barriers to engagement and fostering a sense of community and belonging in online learning environments requires intentional design, innovative pedagogical strategies, and ongoing support for student success.

2. Opportunities
a. Personalized Learning Experiences:

- Online education offers the potential for personalized learning experiences tailored to the individual needs, preferences, and learning styles of students. Adaptive learning technologies, data analytics, and learner-centered pedagogies enable educators to customize instruction, provide targeted support, and promote mastery-based learning.

b. Flexible Delivery Formats:

- The flexibility of online education allows learners to access educational content and engage in learning activities anytime, anywhere, and on any device. Whether balancing work, family, or other commitments, students can pursue their studies at their own pace and on their own schedule, accommodating diverse learning needs and lifestyles.

c. Global Collaboration and Diversity:

- Online education transcends geographical boundaries, connecting learners and educators from diverse cultural backgrounds and perspectives. Through virtual classrooms, collaborative projects, and cross-cultural exchanges, students have the opportunity to broaden their worldview, develop intercultural competencies, and foster global citizenship.

Current Trends and Future Directions in Distance and Online Education

Current Trends:

a. Growth of Massive Open Online Courses (MOOCs):

- MOOCs continue to gain popularity as a scalable and accessible form of online education. Leading platforms like Coursera, edX, and Udacity offer a wide range of courses from top universities and institutions, attracting millions of learners worldwide. MOOCs provide learners with the opportunity to explore diverse subjects, acquire new skills, and earn certifications or micro-credentials at their own pace.

b. Adoption of Virtual Reality (VR) in Education:

- Virtual reality (VR) technology is increasingly being integrated into online education to enhance immersive learning experiences. VR simulations, virtual field trips, and interactive 3D environments offer students the opportunity to engage with course content in innovative ways, fostering deeper understanding and retention of complex concepts. As VR technology becomes more affordable and accessible, its potential to transform online education is being realized across various disciplines and industries.

Future Directions and Potential Innovations:
a. Personalized and Adaptive Learning:

- The future of distance and online education lies in personalized and adaptive learning technologies that cater to the individual needs and preferences of learners. AI-driven algorithms, learning analytics, and intelligent tutoring systems will enable educators to deliver customized learning experiences, provide real-time feedback, and scaffold instruction based on learner progress and performance.

b. Augmented Reality (AR) and Mixed Reality (MR) Integration:

- Augmented reality (AR) and mixed reality (MR) technologies hold promise for revolutionizing online education by overlaying digital content onto the physical world. AR and MR applications can create interactive learning environments, simulate real-world scenarios, and facilitate hands-on learning experiences in diverse fields such as healthcare, engineering, and the arts.

c. Gamification and Digital Badging:

- Gamification techniques and digital badging systems will continue to play a prominent role in online education, incentivizing learner engagement, motivating progress, and recognizing achievement. Game-based learning platforms, quests, challenges, and rewards will enhance learner motivation, promote active participation, and foster a culture of lifelong learning.

II

Foundations of Online Learning

Pedagogical Theories and Models Applicable to Online Education

Overview of Key Pedagogical Theories and Models:

Pedagogical theories provide the foundation for understanding how people learn and inform instructional practices. In the context of online education, several theories and models guide the design and implementation of effective learning experiences. Here are three prominent ones:

1. **Constructivist Learning Theory:**

- Constructivism posits that learners actively construct their own understanding of the world by building upon prior knowledge and experiences. In online education, constructivist principles emphasize learner-centered approaches, collaborative learning environments, and authentic tasks that promote critical thinking and problem-solving skills.

2. **Connectivist Learning Theory:**

   - Connectivism acknowledges the interconnected nature of knowledge and focuses on the role of networks, digital technologies, and distributed learning environments in shaping learning experiences. In online education, connectivist principles emphasize the importance of networked learning, social media, and open educational resources (OER) in facilitating knowledge creation and dissemination in digital environments.

3. **Socio-cultural Learning Theory:**

   - Socio-cultural theory emphasizes the social and cultural context of learning, highlighting the role of social interaction, language, and cultural artifacts in shaping cognitive development. In online education, socio-cultural principles emphasize the importance of social presence, collaborative learning activities, and culturally relevant pedagogies that promote dialogue, negotiation, and shared meaning-making among learners.

Relevance to Online Education:

Each of these theories offers valuable insights into the design and facilitation of online learning experiences:

- **Constructivist Approach:** Online courses can be designed to promote active engagement, self-directed learning, and collaboration among learners. Discussion forums, group projects, and problem-based learning activities can provide opportunities for students to construct knowledge and meaning in digital environments.
- **Connectivist Approach:** Online learning platforms can be leveraged to create networked learning communities where students can connect with peers, experts, and resources across diverse contexts and disciplines. Social media, blogs, wikis, and online forums can facilitate knowledge sharing, collaborative inquiry, and collective problem-solving in distributed learning networks.
- **Socio-cultural Approach:** Online courses can be designed to foster social presence, cultural sensitivity, and community-building among learners from diverse backgrounds. Culturally relevant content, collaborative learning tasks, and synchronous communication tools can promote social interaction, co-construction of knowledge, and the development of a sense of belonging in online learning communities.

Application to Designing Engaging and Effective Online Learning Experiences:

By integrating principles from constructivist, connectivist, and socio-cultural learning theories, online educators can design engaging and effective learning experiences that:

- Foster active participation and collaboration among learners.

- Promote critical thinking, problem-solving, and inquiry-based learning.
- Cultivate a sense of community and belonging in online learning environments.
- Facilitate the creation and sharing of knowledge in digital networks.
- Support diverse learners' needs and preferences through flexible, learner-centered approaches.

Incorporating these theories into online course design can enhance learner engagement, motivation, and achievement, ultimately leading to more meaningful and impactful learning experiences in the digital age.

Principles of Effective Online Teaching and Learning

In the dynamic landscape of online education, effective teaching and learning practices are essential for creating engaging, interactive, and meaningful learning experiences. Here are key principles and best practices for designing and facilitating online courses:

1. Learner-Centered Approaches:

- Design courses with the needs, interests, and preferences of learners at the forefront.
- Offer opportunities for student choice, autonomy, and self-directed learning.
- Provide diverse learning pathways, resources, and activities to accommodate different learning styles and preferences.

2. Active Learning Strategies:

- Engage students actively in the learning process through interactive activities, discussions, and assignments.

- Incorporate problem-solving tasks, case studies, simulations, and real-world applications to promote deeper understanding and retention of concepts.
- Encourage collaborative learning experiences, peer interaction, and knowledge sharing among students.

3. Interaction Design:

- Foster meaningful interactions between students, instructors, and course content.
- Create a supportive online learning community where students feel connected, valued, and engaged.
- Use a variety of communication tools, such as discussion forums, video conferencing, and messaging platforms, to facilitate interaction and collaboration.

4. Instructor Presence:

- Establish a strong instructor presence in the online course to provide guidance, support, and feedback to students.
- Communicate clear expectations, learning objectives, and assessment criteria at the outset of the course.
- Be responsive to student questions, concerns, and feedback, and actively participate in online discussions and activities.

5. Feedback Mechanisms:

- Provide timely and constructive feedback on student progress, performance, and assignments.
- Offer formative feedback to help students identify strengths and areas for improvement throughout the

learning process.
- Use a variety of feedback modalities, including written comments, audio recordings, and video messages, to cater to diverse learner preferences.

6. Social Presence:

- Cultivate a sense of social presence in the online learning environment to promote engagement and collaboration.
- Encourage icebreaker activities, introductions, and informal interactions to help students get to know each other and build rapport.
- Facilitate opportunities for social interaction, peer support, and community-building among students through group projects, team activities, and virtual events.

Understanding the Digital Divide and Accessibility Issues

In the rapidly evolving landscape of online education, addressing the digital divide and accessibility issues is paramount to ensuring equitable access to learning opportunities for all learners. Here's a comprehensive exploration of these challenges and potential strategies for promoting digital inclusion in online learning environments:

1. Exploration of the Digital Divide:

- The digital divide refers to the gap between those who have access to digital technologies and those who do not, creating disparities in access to information, resources, and opportunities.

- Impact on Access to Online Education: The digital divide exacerbates existing inequalities in education, limiting access to online courses, digital learning materials, and virtual learning environments for marginalized populations.

2. Factors Contributing to Digital Inequality:

- Socio-economic Status: Affordability of technology and internet access can be prohibitive for individuals from low-income households, exacerbating disparities in access to online education.
- Geographical Location: Rural and remote areas may lack access to high-speed internet infrastructure, limiting connectivity and hindering participation in online learning.
- Technological Infrastructure: Inadequate technology infrastructure, such as outdated hardware or unreliable internet connections, can pose barriers to accessing online education in certain regions or communities.

3. Strategies for Addressing Digital Divide Challenges:

- Providing Affordable Access: Implement initiatives to increase affordability of technology and internet access, such as subsidized internet plans, discounted devices, and community broadband projects.
- Improving Infrastructure: Invest in expanding and improving technology infrastructure, particularly in underserved rural and remote areas, to ensure reliable internet connectivity and access to digital resources.
- Digital Literacy Training: Offer digital literacy programs and training to equip individuals with the skills and

knowledge needed to navigate online learning platforms, use digital tools effectively, and participate in digital communities.

4. Examination of Accessibility Issues:

- Accessibility in online education refers to ensuring that digital learning materials, platforms, and environments are accessible to all learners, including those with disabilities.
- Barriers Faced by Learners with Disabilities: Common barriers include inaccessible website designs, lack of alternative formats for content (e.g., text transcripts for videos), and limited support for assistive technologies.
- Importance of Inclusive Design: Designing inclusive online learning materials and platforms that are accessible to learners with diverse abilities is essential for promoting equitable access and participation in online education.

5. Strategies for Promoting Digital Inclusion:

- Incorporating Universal Design Principles: Apply universal design principles to online course design and development to ensure that digital learning materials and platforms are accessible to learners with diverse needs and preferences.
- Providing Accessibility Resources: Offer resources, guidelines, and training to educators and instructional designers on creating accessible content and incorporating accessibility features into online courses.
- Engaging Stakeholders: Collaborate with stakeholders, including learners, educators, administrators, and

disability support services, to identify accessibility barriers and develop inclusive solutions that meet the needs of all learners.

III

Technology in Online Education

Learning Management Systems (LMS) and Their Functionalities

Introduction to Learning Management Systems (LMS): Learning Management Systems (LMS) are digital platforms designed to facilitate the delivery, management, and tracking of online courses and educational content. These systems provide a centralized hub for instructors to organize course materials, engage with students, administer assessments, and monitor learner progress.

Overview of LMS Functionalities:

1. **Course Creation and Organization:**

   - LMS platforms allow instructors to create and organize course content, including lectures, readings, assignments, and multimedia resources.

- Course materials can be structured into modules or units, making it easy for students to navigate and access relevant content.

2. **Content Delivery:**

- LMS platforms facilitate the delivery of course content through various formats, such as text documents, videos, audio recordings, presentations, and interactive multimedia.
- Instructors can upload files directly to the LMS or embed content from external sources, providing flexibility in content delivery.

3. **Assessment and Grading:**

- LMS platforms support the creation and administration of assessments, including quizzes, exams, assignments, and discussions.
- Instructors can set parameters for assessments, such as time limits, question types, and grading criteria, and track student performance through the LMS.
- Automated grading features streamline the assessment process, providing immediate feedback to students and reducing administrative burden for instructors.

4. **Communication Tools:**

- LMS platforms offer communication tools to facilitate interaction and collaboration between instructors and students, as well as among peers.

- Features may include announcements, messaging systems, discussion forums, chat rooms, and video conferencing capabilities.
- These tools promote engagement, foster community-building, and provide avenues for academic support and feedback.

5. **Analytics:**

- LMS platforms provide analytics and reporting features that enable instructors to track learner progress, monitor participation, and assess course effectiveness.
- Data metrics may include student activity, engagement levels, assessment scores, completion rates, and learning outcomes.
- Analytics dashboards and reports empower instructors to make data-informed decisions and tailor instructional strategies to meet the needs of individual learners.

Examination of Popular LMS Platforms:

- **Moodle:** Moodle is an open-source LMS known for its flexibility and customization options. It offers a wide range of features, including course management, content creation, assessment tools, communication tools, and reporting capabilities.
- **Canvas:** Canvas is a cloud-based LMS known for its user-friendly interface and intuitive design. It offers robust features for course creation, collaboration, assessment, and analytics, as well as integrations with third-party tools and apps.

- **Blackboard:** Blackboard is a widely used LMS in higher education, known for its comprehensive suite of tools for course management, content delivery, assessment, communication, and collaboration.
- **Google Classroom:** Google Classroom is a popular LMS in K-12 education, seamlessly integrated with Google's suite of productivity tools. It offers features for creating and distributing assignments, providing feedback, and facilitating communication and collaboration among students and teachers.

Virtual Classrooms and Synchronous Learning Tools

Introduction: Virtual classroom platforms and synchronous learning tools facilitate real-time interaction between instructors and students in online learning environments. These tools enable live communication, collaboration, and engagement, replicating the interactive nature of traditional face-to-face classrooms in a digital space.

Overview of Features:

1. **Video Conferencing:** Virtual classroom platforms typically feature video conferencing capabilities, allowing participants to see and hear each other in real-time. Video conferencing enhances instructor presence and promotes engagement by enabling visual and verbal communication.

2. **Live Chat:** Live chat functionalities enable text-based communication between participants during synchronous sessions. Chat features facilitate real-time interaction, Q&A sessions, and group discussions, providing an additional avenue for engagement and participation.

3. **Screen Sharing:** Screen sharing allows instructors to share their screen with participants, enabling them to present slides, documents, applications, or multimedia content. Screen sharing enhances content delivery and facilitates interactive presentations, demonstrations, and collaborative activities.

4. **Whiteboarding:** Some virtual classroom platforms offer whiteboarding tools that allow participants to draw, write, or annotate on a shared virtual whiteboard. Whiteboarding features enable collaborative problem-solving, brainstorming, and visual communication during synchronous sessions.

5. **Polling:** Polling functionalities enable instructors to create and administer polls or surveys to gather feedback, assess understanding, or stimulate discussion among participants. Polling features promote active engagement, interactivity, and participation in virtual classroom environments.

Best Practices for Facilitating Synchronous Online Sessions:

1. **Establish Clear Expectations:** Communicate clear instructions, learning objectives, and expectations for participation at the beginning of each synchronous session.

2. **Engage Students Actively:** Encourage active participation through interactive activities, discussions, polls, and collaborative tasks.

3. **Promote Interaction:** Foster interaction among participants by incorporating opportunities for group discussions, peer interaction, and collaborative problem-solving.

4. **Use Multimedia:** Incorporate multimedia elements such as videos, images, and interactive simulations to enhance engagement and reinforce key concepts.
5. **Provide Timely Feedback:** Offer immediate feedback and guidance to students during synchronous sessions to address questions, clarify misunderstandings, and reinforce learning outcomes.
6. **Manage Time Effectively:** Allocate time strategically, balancing content delivery, interactive activities, and opportunities for reflection and discussion.
7. **Be Responsive:** Be responsive to student questions, concerns, and feedback, and adapt your instruction accordingly to meet the needs of individual learners.
8. **Encourage Participation:** Create a supportive and inclusive learning environment where all participants feel comfortable and encouraged to contribute their ideas and perspectives.

Educational Apps, Simulations, and Gamification in Online Learning

Introduction: Educational apps, simulations, and gamification are powerful tools for enhancing student engagement, motivation, and learning outcomes in online education. These interactive technologies leverage gamified elements, simulations, and immersive experiences to create dynamic and engaging learning environments that promote active participation and foster mastery of course content.

Overview of Educational Apps: Educational apps encompass a wide range of digital tools and resources designed to support learning across various subjects and learning objectives. These apps offer interactive exercises, tutorials, quizzes, games, and other educational activities that cater to different learning styles and preferences. Examples include language learning apps like Duolingo, math apps like Khan Academy, and coding apps like Scratch.

Exploration of Simulations: Virtual simulations provide immersive learning experiences that replicate real-world scenarios and environments, allowing students to explore concepts, practice skills, and solve problems in a safe and interactive manner. Simulations are particularly valuable for STEM education, healthcare training, and technical skills development. Examples include virtual labs for science experiments, flight simulators for pilot training, and medical simulations for surgical procedures.

Discussion on Gamification: Gamification involves the integration of game elements and mechanics into non-game contexts, such as online courses, to enhance engagement, motivation, and learning outcomes. Gamification techniques include points, badges, leaderboards, quests, levels, challenges, and rewards, which encourage active participation, competition, and mastery. Gamified elements can be incorporated into course activities, assessments, and progress tracking systems to incentivize learning and promote a sense of achievement among students.

Best Practices for Integration:

1. **Align with Learning Objectives:** Ensure that educational apps, simulations, and gamification elements align with course objectives and support desired learning outcomes.
2. **Provide Feedback and Guidance:** Offer feedback, guidance, and support to students as they engage with educational apps, simulations, and gamified activities to

promote learning and skill development.

3. **Promote Active Exploration:** Encourage students to actively explore, experiment, and interact with educational apps, simulations, and gamified experiences to deepen their understanding and mastery of course content.

4. **Foster Collaboration:** Facilitate collaboration and peer interaction through multiplayer games, cooperative challenges, and collaborative projects to enhance social learning and teamwork skills.

5. **Monitor Progress and Adjustments:** Monitor student progress, performance, and engagement with educational apps, simulations, and gamified activities, and make adjustments as needed to optimize learning experiences and outcomes.

IV

Designing Online Courses

Course Design Principles and Frameworks

Introduction: Effective online course design is essential for creating engaging, meaningful, and impactful learning experiences for students. By employing foundational principles and instructional design frameworks, educators can design courses that promote student learning, engagement, and success in online environments.

Overview of Instructional Design Models:

1. **ADDIE Model (Analysis, Design, Development, Implementation, Evaluation):**

   - **Analysis:** Identify learning needs, goals, and objectives. Conduct a needs assessment and analyze the characteristics of learners, content, and context.
   - **Design:** Develop a blueprint for the course, including learning objectives, assessments, content, activities,

and instructional strategies.

- **Development:** Create instructional materials and multimedia content based on the design specifications. Develop assessments, activities, and learning resources.
- **Implementation:** Deliver the course to learners using appropriate technologies and instructional methods. Provide support and guidance to facilitate student learning.
- **Evaluation:** Assess the effectiveness of the course in achieving learning objectives and meeting learner needs. Gather feedback from students and stakeholders to inform revisions and improvements.

2. **SAM Model (Successive Approximation Model):**

- The SAM model emphasizes iterative development and rapid prototyping, focusing on continuous feedback and refinement throughout the course design process.
- The process involves three main phases: Preparation, Iterative Design, and Iterative Development.
- In the Preparation phase, designers gather information, define goals, and establish project parameters.
- The Iterative Design phase involves creating prototypes, testing ideas, gathering feedback, and refining the course design based on iterative cycles of review and revision.
- In the Iterative Development phase, designers build, refine, and finalize the course materials based on feedback and insights gained from the design iterations.

Discussion on Key Components of Course Design:

1. **Learning Objectives:** Clearly define measurable learning objectives that articulate what students are expected to know, understand, and be able to do by the end of the course.
2. **Assessments:** Develop a variety of assessments, including formative assessments for ongoing feedback and summative assessments to evaluate student learning outcomes.
3. **Content Sequencing:** Organize course content in a logical and coherent sequence that aligns with learning objectives and promotes comprehension and retention.
4. **Learner Engagement Strategies:** Implement strategies to engage learners actively in the learning process, such as interactive activities, multimedia resources, discussions, and collaborative projects.

Creating Engaging Multimedia Content
Exploration of Strategies for Creating Multimedia Content:

1. **Understand Learning Objectives:** Before creating multimedia content, ensure a clear understanding of learning objectives. Multimedia should align closely with course goals and support desired learning outcomes.
2. **Utilize Variety:** Incorporate a variety of multimedia elements to cater to diverse learning styles and preferences. Mix videos, animations, infographics, interactive simulations, audio recordings, and written text to provide multiple avenues for engagement and comprehension.

3. **Storytelling:** Use storytelling techniques to convey information in a compelling and memorable way. Narratives, case studies, and real-life examples can enhance engagement and help learners connect with the content on a deeper level.

4. **Interactivity:** Include interactive elements to encourage active engagement and participation. Interactive quizzes, simulations, games, and exercises can promote active learning and allow learners to apply knowledge in a practical context.

5. **Visual Design:** Pay attention to visual design principles to create visually appealing multimedia content. Use consistent branding, clear layouts, appropriate colors, and engaging visuals to enhance comprehension and retention.

6. **Accessibility:** Ensure multimedia content is accessible to all learners, including those with disabilities. Provide alternative formats for multimedia content (e.g., captions for videos, transcripts for audio recordings) and design content with accessibility features in mind (e.g., high contrast, readable fonts).

7. **Engage Emotions:** Appeal to learners' emotions to increase engagement and retention. Use storytelling, humor, empathy, and relatable examples to create a connection with learners and evoke emotional responses that enhance learning.

8. **Feedback and Reflection:** Incorporate opportunities for feedback and reflection within multimedia content. Include prompts for learners to pause and reflect on the content, answer questions, or discuss concepts with peers to deepen understanding and promote critical thinking.

Guidance on Selecting Appropriate Multimedia Elements:

1. **Videos:** Use videos to demonstrate complex concepts, present demonstrations or experiments, showcase real-world examples, or provide expert insights and interviews.
2. **Animations:** Utilize animations to illustrate processes, visualize abstract concepts, or simplify complex ideas in a dynamic and engaging way.
3. **Infographics:** Create infographics to present data, statistics, or information in a visually appealing and easy-to-understand format.
4. **Interactive Simulations:** Incorporate interactive simulations to allow learners to explore concepts, manipulate variables, and observe cause-and-effect relationships in a hands-on manner.
5. **Audio Recordings:** Include audio recordings for lectures, presentations, or narrations to accommodate auditory learners and provide alternative modes of content delivery.

Tips for Designing Visually Appealing, Interactive, and Accessible Multimedia Content:

1. **Keep it Simple:** Avoid clutter and overload. Present information in digestible chunks and focus on clarity and simplicity in design.
2. **Use Engaging Visuals:** Incorporate relevant images, graphics, and illustrations to enhance comprehension and capture learners' attention.
3. **Provide Navigation Options:** Include navigation options and clear instructions for interacting with

multimedia content to ensure ease of use and accessibility.

4. **Test for Accessibility:** Test multimedia content for accessibility using assistive technologies and ensure compatibility with screen readers, keyboard navigation, and other accessibility features.

5. **Seek Feedback:** Gather feedback from learners on multimedia content to identify areas for improvement and make adjustments based on user preferences and needs.

Incorporating Interactivity and Collaboration in Online Courses

1. Techniques for Incorporating Interactivity and Collaboration:

- **Polls and Quizzes:** Use polls and quizzes to assess understanding, stimulate discussion, and engage learners actively during synchronous or asynchronous sessions.

- **Discussion Forums:** Incorporate discussion forums to facilitate peer interaction, knowledge sharing, and collaborative problem-solving. Encourage students to ask questions, share insights, and engage in dialogue around course topics.

- **Group Projects:** Assign group projects or collaborative assignments that require students to work together to solve problems, complete tasks, or create deliverables. Group projects promote teamwork, communication, and critical thinking skills.

- **Case Studies:** Present case studies or real-world scenarios that require analysis, synthesis, and application of course concepts. Encourage students to explore multiple perspectives, propose solutions, and engage in critical reflection.

- **Simulations:** Integrate virtual simulations or interactive exercises that simulate real-world environments or scenarios. Simulations allow students to apply theoretical knowledge in practical contexts, make decisions, and observe outcomes.
- **Peer Assessments:** Implement peer assessment activities where students provide feedback and evaluate each other's work based on predefined criteria. Peer assessments promote self-reflection, peer learning, and accountability.

2. Overview of Interactive Learning Activities:

- **Discussions:** Facilitate structured discussions around course topics, readings, or case studies. Encourage active participation, critical thinking, and respectful dialogue among students.
- **Group Projects:** Assign collaborative projects that require students to work together to solve problems, complete tasks, or produce artifacts. Group projects foster teamwork, communication, and collaborative problem-solving skills.
- **Case Studies:** Present real-world case studies or scenarios that challenge students to apply theoretical knowledge to practical situations. Encourage students to analyze information, identify solutions, and justify their reasoning.
- **Simulations:** Integrate interactive simulations or virtual labs that allow students to explore concepts, conduct experiments, and observe outcomes in a controlled environment. Simulations provide hands-on

learning experiences and promote inquiry-based learning.

- **Peer Assessments**: Implement peer assessment activities where students evaluate each other's work and provide constructive feedback. Peer assessments promote critical evaluation skills, self-reflection, and peer learning.

3. Strategies for Leveraging Communication Tools and Collaboration Platforms:

- **Discussion Forums**: Use discussion forums to facilitate asynchronous discussions and peer interaction. Encourage students to ask questions, share insights, and engage in dialogue around course topics.
- **Collaboration Platforms**: Utilize collaboration platforms such as Google Workspace, Microsoft Teams, or Slack to facilitate real-time collaboration, document sharing, and project management among students.

Social Learning Environments: Foster social learning environments by creating opportunities for informal interactions, networking, and community-building. Encourage students to connect with peers, share resources, and support each other outside of formal course activities

V

Teaching Strategies for Online Environments

Facilitating Online Discussions and Group Work:

1. **Establish Clear Guidelines:**

   - Clearly outline expectations and guidelines for online discussions and group work in the course syllabus or assignment instructions.
   - Specify participation requirements, communication norms (e.g., respectful language, constructive feedback), and deadlines for contributions.
   - Provide guidance on how students should engage with each other, respond to prompts, and contribute to the discussion.

2. **Use Structured Prompts:**

- Develop structured discussion prompts or questions that align with learning objectives and course content.
- Provide clear instructions and prompts that prompt critical thinking, reflection, and interaction among students.
- Break down complex topics into manageable discussion topics or themes to guide the conversation.

3. **Encourage Active Participation:**

- Foster active participation by posing open-ended questions that encourage critical thinking and diverse perspectives.
- Facilitate debates or discussions on controversial topics to encourage engagement and critical analysis.
- Prompt students to respond to each other's contributions, ask follow-up questions, and build upon each other's ideas.

4. **Promote Collaboration:**

- Assign roles and responsibilities within groups to distribute tasks and promote accountability.
- Provide resources, guidelines, and support materials to facilitate collaboration and guide group work.
- Foster a supportive team environment by encouraging communication, teamwork, and mutual respect among group members.

5. **Provide Feedback:**

- Monitor online discussions and group work actively to ensure participation and engagement.
- Provide timely and constructive feedback to guide students' contributions, clarify misconceptions, and address any issues or concerns.
- Encourage students to reflect on their contributions and the feedback received, and make adjustments accordingly to improve their participation and collaboration skills.

Providing Feedback and Assessment in Digital Formats:

1. **Use Varied Feedback Methods:**

- Cater to diverse learner preferences by providing feedback in various digital formats, such as:

  - Written comments: Offer detailed feedback and suggestions for improvement in written form.
  - Audio recordings: Provide verbal feedback or explanations using audio recordings to convey tone and nuance.
  - Video feedback: Record video feedback to offer personalized guidance and encouragement.
  - Screen recordings: Use screen recording software to demonstrate concepts or provide step-by-step instructions.

- Offer a combination of these methods to accommodate different learning styles and preferences.

2. **Utilize Rubrics:**

   - Develop clear and transparent grading rubrics that outline assessment criteria, expectations, and performance levels.
   - Use rubrics to provide consistent and constructive feedback on assignments and assessments.
   - Communicate rubric criteria to students in advance to help them understand how their work will be evaluated and what is expected of them.

3. **Offer Formative Feedback:**

   - Provide formative feedback throughout the learning process to support student progress and improvement.
   - Use formative assessments, such as quizzes, practice exercises, or draft submissions, to gauge understanding and identify areas for improvement.
   - Incorporate self-assessments and peer feedback activities to scaffold learning and promote reflection.
   - Encourage students to reflect on feedback received and use it to revise and refine their work.

4. **Leverage Technology:**

   - Take advantage of digital tools and platforms to streamline assessment processes, manage feedback, and track student progress efficiently.
   - Use learning management systems (LMS) to distribute assignments, collect submissions, and provide feedback in a centralized manner.

- Utilize online quizzes, surveys, or assessment tools to assess student understanding and provide immediate feedback.
- Explore grading software or online rubric tools to automate grading and provide consistent feedback across assignments.

5. **Encourage Self-Reflection:**

- Promote self-reflection by encouraging students to assess their own learning progress, strengths, and areas for improvement.
- Provide opportunities for self-assessment and goal-setting to empower students in their learning journey.
- Encourage students to review their own work, compare it against assessment criteria or rubrics, and identify areas where they can improve.
- Foster a growth mindset by emphasizing the importance of learning from mistakes and seeking opportunities for growth and development.

Addressing Challenges in Student Engagement and Motivation:

1. **Create Engaging Content:**

- Design interactive and multimedia-rich content that captures students' interest and enhances engagement.
- Incorporate storytelling, real-world examples, and gamified elements to make learning more compelling and relevant to students' interests.

- Use a variety of multimedia formats, such as videos, animations, infographics, and interactive simulations, to present information in diverse and engaging ways.

2. **Promote Active Learning:**

- Incorporate active learning strategies that require students to actively engage with course materials and participate in learning activities.
- Use case studies, simulations, problem-solving tasks, and collaborative projects to promote critical thinking, problem-solving skills, and knowledge application.
- Provide opportunities for students to apply concepts in real-world contexts and engage in hands-on learning experiences.

3. **Build Community:**

- Foster a sense of community and belonging in the online classroom by creating opportunities for interaction and collaboration among students.
- Use icebreaker activities, virtual meetups, discussion forums, and group projects to encourage peer interaction, collaboration, and support.
- Facilitate peer learning and mentorship opportunities to help students connect with each other and build supportive relationships.

4. **Provide Choice and Autonomy:**

- Offer students flexibility and autonomy in how they engage with course materials and demonstrate their learning.
- Incorporate options for project topics, assessment formats, and learning pathways to accommodate diverse learner preferences and interests.
- Allow students to choose assignments or projects that align with their personal interests or career goals, fostering intrinsic motivation and ownership of learning.

5. **Offer Support:**

- Provide academic and technical support to students as needed to address challenges and ensure success in the online learning environment.
- Offer tutorials, resources, office hours, and online assistance to help students navigate course materials, technology tools, and academic concepts.
- Monitor student progress and engagement closely and intervene promptly to address any issues or concerns that may arise.
- Create a supportive and inclusive learning environment where students feel valued, supported, and empowered to succeed.

VI

Student Support and Success in Online Learning

Online Student Orientation and Support Services

1. Orientation Programs:

- **Purpose:** Online orientation programs aim to acquaint students with the online learning environment, course expectations, and available support services.
- **Components:**

  - Introduction to the Learning Management System (LMS): Provide guided tours and tutorials on how to navigate the LMS, access course materials, submit assignments, and participate in discussions.
  - Course Expectations: Clarify course objectives, expectations, deadlines, and assessment criteria to help students understand what is required to succeed

in the course.
- Support Services Overview: Introduce students to available support services, including technical support, academic advising, library resources, and accessibility services.
- Communication Channels: Inform students about communication channels such as email, discussion forums, and virtual office hours to facilitate interaction with instructors and peers.

- **Delivery**: Orientation programs can be delivered asynchronously through pre-recorded videos, interactive modules, or live webinars to accommodate students' schedules and preferences.

2. Technical Support:

- **Purpose**: Technical support services aim to assist students in navigating technology tools and addressing technical issues encountered during online learning.
- **Services**:

  - Troubleshooting Assistance: Offer helpdesk support to troubleshoot technical issues related to accessing course materials, using the LMS, or utilizing software applications.
  - Tutorials and Resources: Provide tutorials, guides, and FAQs to help students troubleshoot common technical problems independently.
  - Device Compatibility: Ensure that online courses and materials are accessible across different devices and platforms to accommodate students with varying technological setups.

- **Accessibility:** Technical support services should be easily accessible and responsive to students' inquiries, with multiple communication channels available for seeking assistance.

3. Academic Advising:

- **Purpose:** Virtual academic advising services aim to provide guidance and support to students in setting academic goals, selecting courses, and planning their educational journey.
- **Services:**

  - Course Selection: Assist students in selecting appropriate courses based on their academic goals, program requirements, and scheduling constraints.
  - Degree Planning: Help students develop personalized degree plans and academic pathways to ensure timely progression toward graduation.
  - Academic Support: Offer guidance on study strategies, time management skills, and resources for academic success.

- **Appointment Scheduling:** Provide online appointment scheduling tools and virtual advising sessions to facilitate communication between students and academic advisors.

4. Library and Research Support:

- **Purpose:** Library and research support services aim to provide students with access to online library resources, research databases, and virtual reference services to support their research and information literacy skills.

- **Services:**

  - Access to Online Resources: Provide students with access to digital library collections, research databases, e-books, and academic journals for conducting research and accessing course materials.
  - Virtual Reference Services: Offer virtual reference assistance through chat, email, or video conferencing to help students with research inquiries, citation questions, and literature searches.
  - Information Literacy Instruction: Offer online tutorials, workshops, and guides on information literacy skills such as evaluating sources, citing references, and conducting effective research.

5. Accessibility Services:

- **Purpose:** Accessibility services ensure that students with disabilities have equal access to online learning materials, assessments, and technology tools.
- **Accommodations:** Provide accommodations such as alternative formats for course materials, extended time for assessments, accessible learning platforms, and assistive technologies to support students' diverse learning needs.
- **Accessibility Resources:** Offer resources and support services to help students with disabilities navigate online learning environments, including information on accessibility features, adaptive technology, and campus accessibility policies.
- **Accessibility Compliance:** Ensure that online courses and materials comply with accessibility standards and

guidelines (e.g., WCAG) to ensure equal access for all students.

Strategies for Fostering a Sense of Community and Belonging:

1. **Icebreaker Activities:**

   - **Purpose:** Icebreaker activities aim to break the ice and facilitate introductions among students to help them get to know each other and build connections within the online community.
   - **Examples:**

     - Introduction Discussions: Create discussion threads where students can introduce themselves, share their interests, and connect with their peers.
     - Virtual Icebreaker Games: Organize online games or activities that encourage students to interact, collaborate, and build rapport with each other.
     - Multimedia Introductions: Invite students to create multimedia introductions (e.g., videos, presentations) to share personal stories, hobbies, and aspirations with their classmates.

2. **Virtual Meetups:**

   - **Purpose:** Virtual meetups provide opportunities for students to connect in real-time, engage in discussions, and collaborate on academic or social activities.
   - **Examples:**

- Virtual Office Hours: Schedule regular virtual office hours or live chat sessions where students can meet with instructors or peers to ask questions, seek clarification, or discuss course topics.
- Study Groups: Facilitate virtual study groups or study sessions where students can work together, share resources, and review course materials.
- Online Social Events: Organize online social events, such as virtual coffee breaks, game nights, or themed discussions, to foster social interaction and community building.

3. **Discussion Forums:**

- **Purpose:** Discussion forums provide a platform for students to share ideas, ask questions, and engage in meaningful dialogue with their peers and instructors.
- **Best Practices:**

  - Create Active Threads: Seed discussion forums with thought-provoking questions, prompts, or current events to stimulate conversation and encourage participation.
  - Foster Collaboration: Encourage students to respond to each other's posts, ask follow-up questions, and engage in respectful debates or discussions.
  - Facilitate Instructor Involvement: Actively participate in discussion forums by providing feedback, answering questions, and guiding discussions to promote student engagement and

interaction.

4. **Group Projects:**

    - **Purpose:** Group projects promote teamwork, communication, and relationship-building among students by assigning collaborative tasks or activities.
    - **Best Practices:**

        - Clear Expectations: Provide clear guidelines, roles, and expectations for group projects to ensure that all team members understand their responsibilities.
        - Peer Accountability: Encourage peer accountability and collaboration by establishing deadlines, milestones, and mechanisms for team communication and coordination.
        - Reflective Practices: Incorporate opportunities for reflection and peer evaluation to assess individual contributions, provide feedback, and improve teamwork skills.

5. **Feedback and Recognition:**

    - **Purpose:** Providing regular feedback, encouragement, and recognition of student achievements fosters a positive and supportive learning environment and reinforces a sense of belonging.
    - **Best Practices:**

- Timely Feedback: Offer timely and constructive feedback on student contributions, assignments, and assessments to guide their learning progress and reinforce positive behaviors.
- Encouragement and Praise: Acknowledge and celebrate student achievements, milestones, and improvements to boost morale and motivation.
- Peer Recognition: Facilitate peer recognition and appreciation by encouraging students to acknowledge and commend their classmates' contributions, efforts, and successes.

Promoting Self-Regulated Learning and Time Management Skills:

1. **Self-Regulation Strategies:**

   - **Purpose:** Teach students self-regulation strategies and study skills to help them manage their time effectively, set goals, monitor progress, and adapt their learning strategies as needed.
   - **Implementation:**

     - Time Management: Teach techniques such as creating schedules, prioritizing tasks, and breaking larger tasks into smaller, manageable chunks to help students allocate their time efficiently.
     - Goal Setting: Guide students in setting specific, measurable, achievable, relevant, and time-bound (SMART) goals to provide direction and motivation for their learning.

- Metacognition: Encourage students to reflect on their learning processes, identify obstacles or challenges, and develop strategies to overcome them.
- Self-Monitoring: Help students develop awareness of their learning progress by encouraging them to track their performance, monitor their study habits, and adjust their strategies as needed.

2. **Time Management Tools:**

- **Purpose:** Offer time management tools, planners, and resources to help students organize their schedules, prioritize tasks, and maintain a healthy work-life balance.
- **Examples:**

  - Digital Calendars: Provide guidance on using digital calendar apps or platforms to schedule classes, assignments, study sessions, and extracurricular activities.
  - Task Management Apps: Introduce students to task management apps or software tools that allow them to create to-do lists, set reminders, and track progress on assignments.
  - Time Tracking Tools: Recommend time tracking tools or techniques (e.g., Pomodoro Technique) to help students manage their time more effectively and stay focused during study sessions.
  - Time Blocking: Teach students the concept of time blocking, where they allocate specific time slots for different activities or tasks to improve productivity and reduce procrastination.

3. **Goal Setting:**

- **Purpose:** Encourage students to set SMART (Specific, Measurable, Achievable, Relevant, Time-bound) goals for their learning objectives and academic progress.
- **Implementation:**

  - Goal-Setting Exercises: Provide structured activities or assignments that guide students through the process of setting short-term and long-term goals related to their academic, personal, or professional development.
  - Goal Reflection: Incorporate regular opportunities for students to reflect on their progress towards their goals, identify barriers or challenges, and adjust their strategies accordingly.
  - Goal Accountability Partners: Encourage students to share their goals with peers, mentors, or instructors and hold each other accountable for their progress through regular check-ins and mutual support.

4. **Feedback and Reflection:**

- **Purpose:** Provide opportunities for students to reflect on their learning experiences, assess their progress, and identify areas for improvement. Offer constructive feedback and guidance to support their self-reflection and growth.
- **Implementation:**

- Reflective Journals: Assign reflective journal entries or blog posts where students can document their thoughts, experiences, and insights gained from their learning activities.
- Peer Feedback: Incorporate peer feedback activities where students can provide constructive feedback to their classmates and receive insights and perspectives from their peers.
- Instructor Feedback: Offer personalized feedback on student assignments, projects, or assessments that highlights strengths, areas for improvement, and actionable suggestions for further development.
- Goal Progress Reviews: Conduct periodic goal progress reviews where students can reflect on their achievements, challenges, and next steps towards their learning goals.

5. **Peer Support Networks:**

- **Purpose:** Facilitate peer support networks and study groups where students can collaborate, share resources, and hold each other accountable for their learning goals.
- **Implementation:**

  - Virtual Study Groups: Encourage students to form virtual study groups or peer support networks where they can discuss course materials, review concepts, and solve problems together.
  - Peer Accountability Partnerships: Pair students up as accountability partners or study buddies to support each other in staying on track with their

learning goals, checking in regularly, and providing encouragement and motivation.

- Online Discussion Forums: Create dedicated discussion forums or social media groups where students can connect with their peers, ask questions, share resources, and seek advice on academic or personal matters.
- Peer Tutoring Programs: Establish peer tutoring programs where advanced students can volunteer to mentor or tutor their peers in specific subject areas, providing additional academic support and guidance.

VII

Assessment and Evaluation in Online Education

Designing Authentic and Meaningful Assessments:

Purpose: The goal of designing assessments in online education is to create evaluation methods that accurately gauge students' understanding, skills, and competencies while fostering meaningful learning experiences. By designing assessments that are authentic and relevant to the course content, educators can engage students in active learning, promote critical thinking, and facilitate the application of knowledge in real-world contexts.

Strategies:

1. **Authentic Tasks:**

   - **Description:** Assessments should mirror real-world challenges or scenarios relevant to the course content. These tasks allow students to apply their knowledge and skills in practical contexts, promoting deeper understanding and transfer of learning.

- **Implementation:** Design assessments that require students to tackle authentic problems, complete real-world tasks, or engage in activities that simulate professional scenarios. For example, in a business management course, students could analyze case studies, develop business plans, or conduct market research projects that reflect challenges encountered in the field.

2. **Performance-Based Assessments:**

- **Description:** Incorporate assessments that require students to demonstrate their abilities through practical tasks, such as projects, case studies, simulations, or portfolio assessments. These assessments provide opportunities for students to showcase their skills and knowledge in authentic contexts.
- **Implementation:** Design performance-based assessments that require students to apply their learning to solve complex problems, complete hands-on projects, or produce tangible artifacts. For instance, in a programming course, students could be tasked with developing a software application or debugging code to demonstrate their programming proficiency.

3. **Formative Assessments:**

- **Description:** Integrate formative assessments throughout the course to provide ongoing feedback on students' progress. These assessments can take the form of quizzes, discussions, peer reviews, or self-assessments, helping students identify areas for improvement and guiding their learning journey.
- **Implementation:** Implement formative assessments at key points in the learning process to check understanding, reinforce concepts, and address misconceptions. Use a variety of formative assessment techniques, such as low-stakes quizzes, concept maps, or think-pair-share activities, to gauge student comprehension and inform instructional decisions.

4. **Rubrics and Criteria:**

- **Description:** Develop clear assessment criteria and rubrics that outline expectations and criteria for success. Rubrics help students understand what is expected of them and provide transparency in assessment grading.
- **Implementation:** Create rubrics that align with learning objectives and clearly articulate the criteria for evaluating student performance. Include specific descriptors for each level of achievement to guide students in understanding the quality of their work and areas for improvement. Share rubrics with students before assessments to set clear expectations and facilitate self-assessment.

Ensuring Academic Integrity in Online Assessments:

Purpose: Maintaining academic integrity is essential in online education to uphold the credibility and validity of assessments and ensure fairness for all students. By implementing strategies to prevent cheating and promote ethical behavior, educators can uphold academic standards and protect the integrity of the learning environment.

Strategies:

1. **Secure Assessment Environments:**

   - **Description:** Utilize secure online assessment platforms or proctoring tools that monitor students' behavior, verify their identity, and prevent cheating. These tools can include features such as webcam monitoring, screen recording, and lockdown browsers.
   - **Implementation:** Choose assessment platforms or proctoring services that offer robust security features to monitor student activity during online exams. Require students to authenticate their identity using methods such as facial recognition or biometric verification to ensure accountability and deter impersonation.

2. **Designing Varied Assessments:**

   - **Description:** Create assessments that are difficult to cheat on by incorporating diverse question formats, such as open-ended questions, problem-solving tasks, or authentic assessments that require critical thinking and application of knowledge.
   - **Implementation:** Design assessments that assess higher-order thinking skills and cannot be easily

answered by searching for information online or copying from other sources. Incorporate scenario-based questions, case studies, or real-world problems that require students to analyze, synthesize, and apply their understanding in unique contexts.

3. **Promoting Ethical Behavior:**

   - **Description:** Educate students about academic integrity policies, plagiarism, and the consequences of academic dishonesty. Encourage a culture of honesty, integrity, and ethical behavior by discussing the importance of academic integrity and providing resources for students to learn about citation practices and ethical research.
   - **Implementation:** Integrate discussions on academic integrity into course syllabi, orientation sessions, and online modules. Clearly communicate expectations regarding citation, referencing, and academic honesty, and provide examples of proper citation practices. Offer resources such as tutorials, guides, and plagiarism detection tools to support students in upholding academic integrity.

4. **Alternative Assessment Methods:**

   - **Description:** Explore alternative assessment methods that minimize the risk of cheating, such as oral exams, presentations, or collaborative projects. These assessments require active participation and engagement, making it more challenging for students to cheat.

- **Implementation:** Design assessments that assess students' understanding and skills through interactive and collaborative activities. Consider using techniques such as peer assessment, group projects, or student-led discussions to evaluate learning outcomes while fostering collaboration and communication skills.

Using Data Analytics to Improve Teaching and Learning Outcomes:

Purpose: Data analytics offer valuable insights into students' learning behaviors, performance patterns, and engagement levels, allowing educators to make informed decisions to enhance teaching and learning outcomes. By leveraging data analytics, educators can identify areas for improvement, personalize learning experiences, and support student success effectively.

Strategies:

1. **Learning Analytics:**

   - **Description:** Employ learning analytics tools integrated into the learning management system (LMS) to track students' online activity, participation rates, assessment scores, and progress towards learning objectives. Analyzing this data helps educators identify trends and patterns in student behavior and engagement.
   - **Implementation:** Utilize learning analytics dashboards and reports provided by the LMS to monitor student activity and performance metrics in real-time. Analyze data on course access, engagement with course materials, discussion

participation, and assessment results to identify students who may need additional support or intervention.

2. Predictive Analytics:

- **Description:** Utilize predictive analytics models to identify at-risk students who may need additional support or intervention. Early warning indicators, such as low engagement, poor performance, or irregular behavior patterns, can trigger proactive interventions to prevent academic challenges and improve student success.
- **Implementation:** Implement predictive analytics algorithms that analyze historical student data to identify patterns associated with academic success or risk factors for attrition. Use predictive models to generate alerts or notifications for educators when students exhibit behaviors indicative of potential academic challenges, allowing for timely intervention and support.

3. Personalized Learning:

- **Description:** Use student data to personalize learning experiences and provide targeted interventions or adaptive feedback based on individual learning needs, preferences, and performance. Personalized learning pathways can cater to diverse student needs and optimize learning outcomes.
- **Implementation:** Leverage student data to dynamically adjust course content, assignments, and

learning activities based on individual learner profiles, preferences, and performance data. Implement adaptive learning technologies or intelligent tutoring systems that use algorithms to deliver customized learning experiences tailored to each student's strengths, weaknesses, and learning pace.

4. **Continuous Improvement:**

   - **Description:** Analyze data to evaluate the effectiveness of instructional strategies, course materials, and assessment methods. Identifying areas for improvement allows educators to refine teaching practices, optimize course design, and enhance the overall learning experience for students.
   - **Implementation:** Conduct regular data-driven evaluations of teaching practices, course materials, and student outcomes to identify areas for improvement. Use feedback from learning analytics, student surveys, and assessments to inform instructional decisions, make adjustments to course content or delivery methods, and implement evidence-based practices to enhance teaching effectiveness and learning outcomes.

VIII

Professional Development for Online Educators

Training and Resources for Transitioning to Online Teaching:

Purpose: The purpose of providing training and resources for transitioning to online teaching is to empower educators with the necessary skills and knowledge to effectively navigate the digital landscape, enabling them to create engaging and meaningful online learning experiences for their students.

Components:

1. **Pedagogical Training:**

   - **Description:** Pedagogical training focuses on imparting educators with the principles and strategies essential for effective online instruction.

This includes understanding the nuances of online course design, facilitating engaging discussions, and employing techniques to foster student engagement in virtual environments.

- **Content:**

  - Principles of Online Course Design: Educators learn about the key principles of instructional design tailored for online learning environments, such as organizing content, setting learning objectives, and designing assessments.
  - Strategies for Facilitating Online Discussions: Educators are equipped with strategies to effectively facilitate online discussions, promote student participation, and maintain a collaborative learning atmosphere.
  - Techniques for Engaging Students: Educators explore various techniques, such as multimedia integration, interactive activities, and gamification, to enhance student engagement and motivation in online courses.

2. **Technical Skills Development:**

- **Description:** Technical skills development provides educators with the proficiency to navigate online learning platforms, utilize digital tools, and leverage educational technology effectively in their teaching practices.
- **Content:**

  - Familiarization with Learning Management Systems (LMS): Educators learn how to navigate popular learning management systems (e.g., Moodle, Canvas, Blackboard) to manage course content, assignments, and communication with students.

- Digital Tools and Educational Technology: Educators are introduced to a variety of digital tools and educational technology solutions, such as video conferencing platforms, interactive whiteboards, and online collaboration tools, to enhance the online learning experience.

- Multimedia Integration: Educators gain skills in creating and integrating multimedia elements, such as videos, presentations, and interactive simulations, to enhance course content and engage learners effectively.

3. **Content Creation:**

- **Description:** Content creation training focuses on guiding educators in developing and adapting course materials for online delivery, ensuring they are accessible, engaging, and aligned with learning objectives.

- **Content:**

  - Creating Multimedia Content: Educators learn techniques for creating multimedia content, such as videos, audio recordings, and interactive presentations, to enhance the delivery of course materials and cater to diverse learning preferences.

  - Designing Interactive Activities: Educators explore strategies for designing interactive activities, such as quizzes, discussions, and simulations, to promote active learning and facilitate student interaction in online courses.

- Ensuring Accessibility: Educators are provided with guidance on ensuring accessibility in online course materials, including designing content that is compatible with assistive technologies, providing alternative formats, and adhering to accessibility standards.

4. **Support Resources:**

- **Description:** Support resources offer educators access to online tutorials, guides, best practices, and instructional videos to assist them throughout their transition to online teaching and address any challenges they may encounter.
- **Content:**

  - Online Tutorials and Guides: Educators have access to comprehensive online tutorials and guides that cover various aspects of online teaching, including using learning management systems, implementing effective instructional strategies, and troubleshooting technical issues.
  - Best Practices: Educators are provided with a repository of best practices and exemplar resources for online teaching, curated from experienced educators and instructional designers, to serve as models for designing and delivering effective online courses.
  - Instructional Videos: Educators can access instructional videos that demonstrate key

concepts, techniques, and strategies related to online teaching, offering visual demonstrations and step-by-step guidance on implementing effective practices.

Ongoing Professional Development Opportunities:

Purpose: The purpose of offering ongoing professional development opportunities is to cultivate a culture of continuous learning and professional growth among online educators. These opportunities are designed to address evolving needs and emerging trends in online education, ensuring educators remain current, innovative, and effective in their teaching practices.

Strategies:

1. **Workshops and Webinars:**

   - **Description:** Workshops, webinars, and seminars provide educators with interactive and focused learning experiences on topics relevant to online teaching. These sessions offer opportunities to explore effective online communication strategies, innovative assessment techniques, inclusive teaching practices, and emerging trends in online education.
   - **Benefits:**

     - Accessibility: Workshops and webinars can be conducted online, making them accessible to educators regardless of their geographical location or scheduling constraints.
     - Expertise Sharing: Educators have the opportunity to learn from experts in the field and gain insights into best practices and innovative

approaches to online teaching.

- Peer Interaction: These sessions facilitate peer interaction and networking, allowing educators to share experiences, exchange ideas, and collaborate with colleagues in similar roles or disciplines.

2. **Online Courses and Certifications:**

- **Description:** Online courses, certifications, and micro-credentials enable educators to deepen their knowledge and skills in specific areas of online education, such as blended learning, instructional design, educational technology, or specialized subject areas.
- **Benefits:**

  - Flexible Learning: Online courses offer flexibility in terms of pacing, scheduling, and learning environment, allowing educators to engage in professional development at their own pace and convenience.
  - Specialized Training: Certifications and micro-credentials provide educators with targeted training in niche areas of online education, enhancing their expertise and credibility in specific domains.
  - Continuous Skill Development: By enrolling in ongoing online courses or pursuing certifications, educators can continuously develop their skills, stay updated on the latest trends and technologies, and adapt to evolving demands in online teaching.

3. **Communities of Practice:**

- **Description:** Communities of practice are collaborative spaces where educators with shared interests, roles, or goals come together to share resources, exchange insights, and support each other's professional development in online teaching.
- **Benefits:**

  - Peer Support: Communities of practice offer a supportive environment where educators can seek advice, share experiences, and receive feedback from peers facing similar challenges and opportunities in online education.
  - Knowledge Sharing: Educators have the opportunity to exchange resources, best practices, lesson plans, and instructional materials related to online teaching, enriching their teaching practices and expanding their repertoire of strategies.
  - Professional Networking: These communities facilitate professional networking and collaboration, fostering connections with colleagues, mentors, and experts in the field of online education.

4. **Conference Attendance:**

- **Description:** Virtual conferences, symposiums, and professional development events focused on online education provide educators with opportunities to engage in keynote presentations, panel discussions, workshops, and networking sessions.

- **Benefits:**

  - Knowledge Exchange: Conferences offer a platform for educators to learn about current trends, research findings, innovative practices, and cutting-edge technologies in online education from leading experts and practitioners.
  - Professional Development: Attending conferences allows educators to gain new insights, perspectives, and ideas to enhance their teaching practices and stay abreast of advancements in the field of online education.
  - Networking Opportunities: Virtual conferences provide opportunities for educators to connect with peers, establish collaborations, and build professional relationships with like-minded individuals in the online education community.

Reflective Practices and Communities of Practice for Online Educators:

Purpose: The purpose of encouraging reflective practices and cultivating communities of practice for online educators is to foster a culture of continuous improvement and professional growth. These strategies provide educators with opportunities to engage in critical reflection, share experiences, and collaborate with peers to enhance their teaching effectiveness and improve student learning outcomes in the online environment.

Strategies:

1. **Reflective Journals and Portfolios:**

- **Description:** Educators are encouraged to maintain reflective journals or portfolios where they document their teaching experiences, successes, challenges, and lessons learned in the online classroom. Regular reflection promotes self-awareness, professional growth, and continuous improvement.
- **Benefits:**

  - Self-Awareness: Reflective practices encourage educators to critically evaluate their teaching methods, instructional strategies, and interactions with students, leading to increased self-awareness and insight into their teaching effectiveness.
  - Professional Growth: By documenting their experiences and reflecting on their teaching practices, educators can identify areas for improvement, set goals for professional development, and implement strategies to enhance their teaching effectiveness over time.
  - Continuous Improvement: Reflective journals and portfolios serve as a repository of insights, reflections, and lessons learned, enabling educators to track their progress, celebrate successes, and learn from past experiences to inform future teaching practices.

2. **Peer Observation and Feedback:**

  - **Description:** Facilitate peer observation programs where educators have the opportunity to observe each other's online teaching sessions and provide constructive feedback and recommendations for improvement. Peer collaboration fosters a culture of trust, support, and collegiality.

- **Benefits:**

  - Professional Dialogue: Peer observation and feedback provide educators with opportunities to engage in professional dialogue, share perspectives, and exchange insights on effective teaching practices in the online classroom.
  - Constructive Feedback: Educators receive constructive feedback from peers on their teaching methods, instructional strategies, and communication techniques, helping them identify strengths and areas for improvement in their online teaching practices.
  - Collaborative Learning: Peer observation programs promote collaboration and mutual learning among educators, allowing them to learn from each other's experiences, experiment with new teaching approaches, and collectively enhance the quality of online instruction.

3. **Online Educator Networks:**

- **Description:** Establish online educator networks or communities of practice where educators can connect, share resources, discuss emerging trends, and seek advice on teaching-related issues. These communities provide opportunities for collaborative problem-solving, knowledge sharing, and professional networking.
- **Benefits:**

- Resource Sharing: Online educator networks facilitate the sharing of resources, best practices, lesson plans, and instructional materials among educators, enriching teaching practices and expanding educators' repertoire of strategies.
- Peer Support: Educators can seek advice, share experiences, and receive support from peers facing similar challenges and opportunities in online education, fostering a sense of belonging and camaraderie within the online educator community.
- Professional Networking: Online educator networks provide opportunities for educators to build professional relationships, establish collaborations, and connect with like-minded individuals in the online education community, enhancing their professional network and visibility within the field.

4. **Professional Learning Communities (PLCs):**

- **Description:** Form professional learning communities focused on specific areas of online education, such as digital literacy, student engagement, or assessment practices. PLCs offer a structured framework for ongoing collaboration, professional development, and collective learning.
- **Benefits:**

  - Specialized Focus: PLCs allow educators to delve deeper into specific areas of online education, share expertise, and exchange insights on best practices, emerging trends, and research findings in their respective domains.

- Supportive Environment: Professional learning communities provide a supportive environment where educators can seek advice, brainstorm ideas, and collaborate on projects related to their shared interests or professional goals, fostering a sense of community and mutual support.
- Collective Learning: PLCs promote collective learning and knowledge co-construction, enabling educators to leverage diverse perspectives, experiences, and expertise to address complex challenges and advance their understanding of effective teaching practices in online education.

IX

Policy and Institutional Considerations

Legal and Ethical Issues in Online Education:

Description: Online education presents a myriad of legal and ethical considerations that educators and institutions must navigate to ensure the rights and interests of all stakeholders are protected. These considerations encompass various areas such as privacy, intellectual property, accessibility, and compliance with relevant laws and regulations.

Privacy Concerns:

- In online education, students' personal information, academic records, and communication data are stored and processed digitally. Therefore, ensuring the privacy and security of this sensitive information is paramount.

- Institutions must comply with data protection laws such as the Family Educational Rights and Privacy Act (FERPA) in the United States, which governs the access and disclosure of students' educational records.
- Educators and institutions should implement robust data security measures, such as encryption protocols, secure authentication methods, and regular security audits, to safeguard students' personal data from unauthorized access or breaches.

Intellectual Property Rights:

- Online education involves the creation and distribution of digital learning materials, which may include text, multimedia content, software, and interactive resources. Protecting the intellectual property rights of content creators and respecting copyright laws is essential.
- Educators should be aware of copyright regulations and obtain appropriate permissions or licenses for using third-party materials in their online courses. They should also educate students on copyright compliance and fair use principles.
- Institutions may establish intellectual property policies that outline ownership rights, usage permissions, and guidelines for creating and sharing educational content in online environments.

Accessibility Requirements:

- Online education should be accessible to all students, including those with disabilities, to ensure equal opportunities for learning.

- Institutions should adhere to accessibility standards such as the Web Content Accessibility Guidelines (WCAG) to design digital content, websites, and learning platforms that are perceivable, operable, and understandable for individuals with disabilities.
- Educators should provide alternative formats, accommodations, and assistive technologies to support students with diverse learning needs and ensure they can fully participate in online courses.

Compliance with Regulations:

- Online education providers must comply with relevant laws and regulations governing distance learning, digital communication, and educational technology.
- In addition to FERPA, institutions may need to adhere to other regulations such as the Americans with Disabilities Act (ADA), Section 508 of the Rehabilitation Act, and the Children's Online Privacy Protection Act (COPPA) when delivering online education to specific populations.
- Educators and institutions should stay informed about evolving legal requirements and regularly review and update their policies and practices to ensure compliance with applicable regulations.

Implementation:

- To ensure compliance with legal and ethical standards in online education, educators and institutions should develop comprehensive policies, guidelines, and procedures addressing privacy protection, intellectual property rights, accessibility accommodations, and regulatory compliance.

- Institutions should provide training and resources to educate faculty, staff, and students about their rights and responsibilities regarding privacy, copyright, accessibility, and other legal and ethical issues in online education.
- Collaborating with legal experts, privacy professionals, and accessibility specialists can help institutions develop robust frameworks and protocols for managing legal and ethical considerations in online education effectively.
- Regular audits, assessments, and reviews of institutional practices, data security measures, and accessibility features can help identify areas for improvement and ensure ongoing compliance with legal and ethical standards.

Accreditation and Quality Assurance Standards:

Description: Accreditation and quality assurance play a crucial role in ensuring the credibility, rigor, and effectiveness of online education programs and courses. Accreditation involves the evaluation and recognition of educational institutions or programs by authorized accrediting bodies, while quality assurance encompasses mechanisms and processes to maintain and enhance the quality of educational offerings.

Examination of Accreditation:

- Accreditation for online education programs and courses may be conducted by regional accrediting agencies, national accrediting bodies, or specialized accrediting organizations depending on the jurisdiction and type of institution.

- Accreditation verifies that an institution or program meets established standards of quality, including faculty qualifications, curriculum design, student support services, learning outcomes assessment, and financial stability.
- Accreditation enhances the credibility and reputation of online education offerings, signaling to students, employers, and stakeholders that the program meets recognized standards of excellence.

Importance of Accreditation:

- Accreditation is essential for ensuring the quality and integrity of online education programs and courses. It provides assurance to students that they are receiving a high-quality education that is recognized and respected by employers and other educational institutions.
- Accreditation also facilitates transferability of credits, eligibility for financial aid, and recognition of credentials, enhancing opportunities for students to pursue further education or career advancement.

Implementation of Accreditation Process:

- Institutions seeking accreditation for their online education programs must undergo a rigorous evaluation process conducted by accrediting agencies. This process typically involves self-assessment, external review, site visits, and documentation of compliance with accreditation standards.
- Institutions should familiarize themselves with accreditation requirements, criteria, and best practices specific to online education, which may include

considerations such as faculty qualifications for online teaching, student support services in virtual environments, and technology infrastructure for online delivery.

- Institutions should develop comprehensive accreditation dossiers that demonstrate compliance with accreditation standards and provide evidence of the quality and effectiveness of their online education programs. This may involve documenting student learning outcomes, assessment results, faculty credentials, course materials, and program resources.
- Institutions should actively engage in quality assurance processes, such as peer review, benchmarking, and continuous improvement, to maintain and enhance the quality of their online education offerings over time.

Quality Assurance Mechanisms:

- Quality assurance mechanisms for online education programs may include peer review of course materials and assessments, benchmarking against industry standards or best practices, and ongoing evaluation of student learning outcomes.
- Continuous improvement processes involve collecting and analyzing data on student performance, course effectiveness, and program outcomes to identify areas for enhancement and implement evidence-based interventions to improve teaching and learning.

Conclusion: Accreditation and quality assurance are essential components of ensuring the credibility, rigor, and effectiveness of online education programs and courses. By adhering to accreditation standards and implementing quality assurance mechanisms, institutions can maintain high standards of quality and provide students with a valuable and reputable online learning experience.

Institutional Strategies for Supporting Online Education Initiatives:

Description: Institutions aiming to establish, maintain, and enhance online education initiatives must devise comprehensive strategies. These strategies should encompass various aspects such as securing leadership commitment, providing faculty support, investing in infrastructure, and engaging in strategic planning to ensure the success and sustainability of online education efforts.

Leadership Commitment:

- **Securing Buy-In:** Leadership commitment is crucial for garnering institutional support for online education initiatives. Senior leaders, including university presidents, deans, and department heads, should endorse and advocate for online education as a strategic priority.
- **Resource Allocation:** Leaders must allocate sufficient financial and human resources to support the development, implementation, and continuous improvement of online education programs. This includes funding for faculty training, instructional design support, technological infrastructure, and student support services.

Faculty Support:

- **Professional Development:** Institutions should offer comprehensive professional development opportunities to equip faculty with the knowledge and skills required for effective online teaching. Training programs should cover pedagogical best practices, technology integration, course design principles, and online assessment strategies.

- **Recognition and Incentives:** Recognizing and rewarding faculty contributions to online education is essential for fostering faculty engagement and motivation. Institutions should provide incentives such as stipends, awards, and opportunities for career advancement to encourage faculty participation in online education initiatives.

Infrastructure Investment:

- **Technological Infrastructure:** Institutions must invest in robust technological infrastructure to support online education delivery. This includes acquiring and maintaining state-of-the-art learning management systems (LMS), video conferencing platforms, multimedia development tools, and accessibility resources.
- **Accessibility:** Ensuring accessibility is paramount in online education. Institutions should invest in tools and resources to make online courses accessible to all students, including those with disabilities. This may involve providing captioning services, screen readers, alternative formats for course materials, and accessible design templates.

Strategic Planning:

- **Goal Setting:** Institutions should engage in strategic planning to set clear goals, objectives, and timelines for online education initiatives. Strategic plans should outline the institution's vision for online education, target student populations, program offerings, enrollment targets, and quality assurance measures.
- **Collaboration and Coordination:** Strategic planning should involve collaboration and coordination among different institutional stakeholders, including academic departments, administrative units, IT services, and student support services. Cross-functional teams can ensure that online education initiatives align with institutional priorities and goals.

Implementation:

- **Policy Development:** Institutions should develop clear policies and guidelines governing online education initiatives. These policies should address key areas such as course development and approval processes, intellectual property rights, student privacy, academic integrity, and accessibility compliance.
- **Resource Allocation:** Adequate resource allocation is essential for the successful implementation of online education initiatives. Institutions should allocate funding for faculty training programs, instructional design support, technological infrastructure upgrades, and student support services tailored to online learners.
- **Stakeholder Engagement:** Institutions should engage stakeholders, including faculty, students, administrators, alumni, employers, and accrediting bodies, in the development and implementation of online education initiatives. Regular communication,

feedback mechanisms, and collaboration opportunities can ensure that online education efforts meet the needs and expectations of all stakeholders.

X

Future Trends and Innovations

Emerging Technologies and Their Potential Impact on Online Learning:
Artificial Intelligence (AI):

- **Description**: Artificial intelligence (AI) holds immense potential to transform online learning by offering personalized instruction, automating administrative tasks, and delivering real-time feedback to students.
- **Applications:**

  - *Personalized Instruction:* AI-powered algorithms can analyze student data and learning preferences to tailor instruction to individual needs, ensuring that each student receives content and support suited to their abilities and learning style.
  - *Administrative Automation:* AI can streamline administrative tasks such as grading, scheduling, and

course management, freeing up educators' time to focus on teaching and mentoring students.

- *Real-time Feedback:* AI-driven chatbots and virtual tutors can provide immediate feedback to students, answering questions, clarifying concepts, and offering guidance in real-time.

Virtual Reality (VR) and Augmented Reality (AR):

- **Description:** VR and AR technologies offer immersive and interactive learning experiences that simulate real-world environments, enhancing student engagement and understanding.
- **Applications:**

  - *Immersive Experiences:* VR and AR can create virtual labs, simulations, and field trips that allow students to explore complex concepts and scenarios in a realistic and interactive way.
  - *Hands-on Learning:* VR and AR applications enable students to engage in hands-on learning activities, such as virtual dissections, chemistry experiments, or architectural design projects, without the need for physical materials or equipment.
  - *Spatial Understanding:* AR overlays digital information onto the physical world, providing contextualized learning experiences that help students develop spatial reasoning and problem-solving skills.

Blockchain:

- **Description:** Blockchain technology offers a secure and transparent way to record and verify academic credentials, certifications, and achievements, enhancing the credibility and portability of online credentials.
- **Applications:**

  - *Credential Verification:* Blockchain-based platforms can create tamper-proof records of academic achievements, allowing employers and educational institutions to verify the authenticity of credentials quickly and securely.
  - *Decentralized Credentials:* Blockchain technology enables individuals to own and control their academic records, eliminating the need for intermediaries and reducing the risk of fraud or misrepresentation.
  - *Global Credentialing:* Blockchain-based credentials are portable across borders and institutions, making it easier for learners to access educational opportunities and career pathways worldwide.

Internet of Things (IoT):

- **Description:** The Internet of Things (IoT) encompasses smart sensors, wearables, and connected devices that collect data on student behavior, engagement, and performance, enabling personalized learning experiences and predictive analytics.
- **Applications:**

  - *Data-driven Insights:* IoT devices gather real-time data on student interactions with online learning platforms, providing insights into engagement levels, learning preferences, and performance metrics.

- *Personalized Learning:* AI algorithms can analyze IoT data to personalize learning experiences, recommending content, activities, and interventions tailored to individual student needs and learning trajectories.
- *Early Intervention:* Predictive analytics derived from IoT data can identify at-risk students and alert educators to intervene early with targeted support and resources to prevent academic challenges and improve student success.

Trends in Online Education Research and Practice: Learner-Centered Approaches:

- **Description:** There is a shift towards learner-centered pedagogies in online education, emphasizing student engagement, autonomy, and agency in the learning process.
- **Research Focus:**

  - *Instructional Design:* Research is exploring effective instructional design strategies that prioritize active learning, problem-solving, and inquiry-based approaches in online courses. This includes designing learning activities that promote critical thinking, creativity, and collaboration among students.
  - *Feedback Mechanisms:* Studies are investigating the role of feedback in online learning environments, examining how timely, constructive feedback can enhance student motivation, self-regulation, and learning outcomes. Research is also exploring

innovative feedback mechanisms such as peer feedback, self-assessment, and automated feedback systems.

- *Collaborative Learning:* Research is exploring the benefits of collaborative learning strategies in online environments, such as group projects, peer learning communities, and collaborative problem-solving activities. Studies are examining how collaborative approaches can foster social interaction, knowledge construction, and deeper understanding among students.

Social and Emotional Learning (SEL):

- **Description:** There is a growing recognition of the importance of addressing social and emotional factors in online education to support students' holistic development.
- **Research Focus:**

  - *Integration of SEL Competencies:* Research is exploring ways to integrate social and emotional learning (SEL) competencies such as self-awareness, empathy, and resilience into online curriculum and instruction. Studies are investigating the impact of SEL interventions on student well-being, motivation, and academic success in online learning environments.
  - *Supporting Student Well-being:* Research is examining strategies to promote student well-being and mental health in online education, including mindfulness practices, stress management techniques, and peer support networks. Studies are investigating the effectiveness of online interventions in reducing

stress, anxiety, and burnout among students.

- *Cultivating Online Communities*: Research is focusing on building supportive online communities that foster positive relationships, belonging, and connectedness among students. Studies are exploring the role of social presence, instructor feedback, and peer interaction in creating a sense of community and support in online learning environments.

Accessibility and Inclusivity:

- **Description**: Research is addressing the need to enhance accessibility and inclusivity in online education to ensure equitable access for diverse learners.
- **Research Focus:**

  - *Accessible Course Materials*: Studies are investigating strategies for designing and developing accessible course materials, including text alternatives for multimedia content, navigation aids for screen readers, and keyboard shortcuts for navigation. Research is exploring the impact of accessible design on learner engagement, comprehension, and retention.
  - *Design Guidelines*: Research is developing design guidelines and best practices for creating inclusive online learning environments that accommodate diverse learner needs, preferences, and abilities. This includes recommendations for designing flexible course structures, providing multiple means of representation, and offering alternative assessment formats.

- *Assistive Technologies:* Studies are evaluating the effectiveness of assistive technologies such as screen readers, speech-to-text software, and captioning tools in supporting learners with disabilities in online education. Research is also examining barriers to access and usability issues faced by learners with disabilities in online learning environments and proposing solutions to address these challenges.

Speculation on the Future Direction of Distance and Online Education:
Hybrid Learning Models:

- **Description:** The future of online education may see the widespread adoption of hybrid learning models that blend online and face-to-face instruction, offering flexible and personalized learning experiences.
- **Key Aspects:**

  - *Flexibility and Personalization:* Hybrid learning models allow for flexibility in learning, enabling students to access course materials and engage in activities online at their own pace and convenience while also benefiting from in-person interactions and support.
  - *Combination of Modalities:* Institutions may adopt hybrid approaches that combine synchronous and asynchronous learning activities, virtual classroom sessions, and in-person workshops or labs to create a balanced learning experience that leverages the strengths of both online and traditional modalities.
  - *Diverse Needs and Preferences:* Hybrid learning caters to the diverse needs and preferences of students,

accommodating different learning styles, schedules, and life circumstances. It provides options for students to choose the mode of instruction that best suits their individual needs and preferences.

Global Collaboration and Mobility:

· **Description:** Online education has the potential to facilitate global collaboration and mobility by overcoming geographical barriers and enabling access to high-quality educational resources from anywhere in the world.
· **Key Aspects:**

  · *Breaking Down Borders:* Online education transcends geographical boundaries, allowing students to participate in courses, collaborate with peers, and engage with instructors from diverse cultural backgrounds and locations.
  · *International Partnerships:* The future of online education may involve increased collaboration and partnerships between institutions across borders, fostering cross-cultural exchanges, joint research projects, and collaborative initiatives aimed at addressing global challenges.
  · *Mobility and Access:* Online education provides opportunities for students to access educational opportunities and resources from remote or underserved areas, enhancing mobility and democratizing access to higher education and lifelong learning.

Continuous Innovation and Adaptation:

- **Description:** The landscape of distance and online education is characterized by continuous innovation and adaptation, driven by advances in technology, changes in learner preferences, and shifts in educational paradigms.
- **Key Aspects:**

  - *Technological Advances:* The future of online education will be shaped by technological innovations such as artificial intelligence, virtual reality, and blockchain, which will enhance the effectiveness, efficiency, and accessibility of online learning experiences.
  - *Pedagogical Evolution:* Online education will continue to evolve in response to changing pedagogical trends and educational research, with a growing emphasis on learner-centered approaches, active learning strategies, and social-emotional learning competencies.
  - *Societal Needs and Challenges:* Online education will play a critical role in addressing societal needs and challenges, such as workforce development, lifelong learning, and the democratization of education, by providing flexible, scalable, and inclusive learning solutions.

XI
Conclusion

Summary of Key Insights and Takeaways: Throughout our exploration of distance and online education, several key insights and takeaways have emerged:

1. **Definition and Historical Evolution:** We've defined distance and online education as methods of delivering instruction to students who are not physically present in a traditional classroom setting. Tracing its roots back to correspondence courses and early forms of distance learning, we've witnessed its evolution into the digital age with the advent of the internet and digital technologies.

2. **Key Concepts and Pedagogical Theories:** Understanding concepts such as asynchronous and synchronous learning, blended learning, and virtual learning environments is crucial. We've explored pedagogical theories like constructivism, connectivism, and socio-cultural learning, highlighting their relevance in designing effective online learning experiences.

3. **Technological Advancements**: The digital revolution has transformed online education, democratizing access to learning and expanding educational opportunities globally. We've discussed how emerging technologies like AI, VR, and IoT are shaping the future of online learning, offering personalized, immersive, and data-driven educational experiences.

4. **Challenges and Opportunities**: Despite its benefits, online education also faces challenges related to equity, access, and quality. We've identified opportunities for personalized learning, flexible delivery formats, and global collaboration, emphasizing the need to address challenges proactively while harnessing the potential of online education to overcome traditional barriers to learning.

5. **Legal and Ethical Considerations**: Legal and ethical issues, including privacy concerns, intellectual property rights, and accessibility requirements, must be addressed to ensure the integrity and fairness of online education. Compliance with regulations such as FERPA and ADA is essential in safeguarding students' rights and interests.

6. **Accreditation and Institutional Strategies**: Accreditation and quality assurance standards play a vital role in ensuring the credibility and quality of online education offerings. Institutions must develop policies, allocate resources, and establish infrastructure to support online education initiatives effectively, including faculty development, technology integration, and student support services.

7. **Future Trends and Innovations**: Looking ahead, hybrid learning models, global collaboration, and continuous innovation are shaping the future of distance and online

education. By embracing learner-centered approaches, leveraging emerging technologies, and promoting accessibility and inclusivity, online education has the potential to transform learning experiences and empower learners worldwide.

Call to Action for Advancing Online Education: The call to action for advancing online education is rooted in the recognition of its transformative potential and the collective responsibility of educators, institutions, policymakers, and stakeholders to realize this vision. Here's a detailed explanation of the components involved:

1. **Commitment to Innovation:** Embracing innovation involves adopting new pedagogical approaches, leveraging emerging technologies, and exploring creative solutions to enhance online learning experiences. Educators should be encouraged to experiment with innovative teaching methods, such as flipped classrooms, experiential learning, and project-based assessments, to engage students and promote deeper learning.

2. **Embrace Inclusivity:** Inclusivity lies at the heart of effective online education, ensuring that learners from diverse backgrounds and abilities have equitable access to educational opportunities. Educators should prioritize accessibility in course design, making learning materials and platforms accessible to learners with disabilities. Additionally, efforts should be made to address digital divides and ensure that all learners have the necessary resources and support to succeed in online learning environments.

3. **Continuous Improvement:** Continuous improvement involves ongoing reflection, evaluation, and adaptation to enhance the quality and effectiveness of online education initiatives. Institutions should establish mechanisms for gathering feedback from students and faculty to identify areas for improvement and implement evidence-based practices. Professional development opportunities should be provided to educators to stay abreast of emerging trends and best practices in online teaching and learning.

4. **Investment in Faculty Development and Infrastructure:** Institutions must invest in faculty development programs to equip educators with the knowledge, skills, and resources needed to excel in online teaching. This includes training on instructional design, technology integration, assessment strategies, and pedagogical approaches tailored to the online environment. Furthermore, institutions should allocate resources to develop and maintain robust technological infrastructure, including learning management systems, digital tools, and technical support services, to ensure a seamless online learning experience for students and faculty alike.

5. **Policy Support and Funding:** Policymakers play a critical role in shaping the regulatory framework and funding mechanisms that govern online education. They should prioritize policies that promote innovation, quality assurance, and equitable access to online education. This may include establishing standards for online course quality, providing financial incentives for institutions to invest in online education, and supporting research initiatives to advance the field.

Final Thoughts on the Future of Distance and Online Learning:

The future of distance and online learning is indeed promising, with the potential to revolutionize education on a global scale. Here's a detailed exploration of the final thoughts on the future of distance and online learning:

1. **Expanding Access to Education**: Online education has the power to break down geographical barriers and provide access to quality education for learners around the world. By offering flexible and convenient learning opportunities, online education enables individuals to pursue their educational goals while balancing other responsibilities such as work, family, or personal commitments. This increased access to education has the potential to democratize learning and empower learners from diverse backgrounds to unlock their full potential.

2. **Fostering Lifelong Learning**: Lifelong learning is essential in today's rapidly changing world, where new skills and knowledge are constantly being demanded. Online education offers a platform for individuals to engage in continuous learning and skill development throughout their lives. By offering a wide range of courses, programs, and learning resources, online education supports individuals in adapting to evolving career demands, exploring new interests, and staying competitive in the job market.

3. **Addressing Global Challenges**: Online education has the capacity to address pressing global challenges, such as access to quality education, workforce development, and sustainability. By leveraging technology and innovation, online learning can facilitate collaborative

problem-solving, knowledge sharing, and capacity building across borders. Online education initiatives focused on areas such as sustainable development, healthcare, and social justice have the potential to drive positive social change and contribute to a more equitable and sustainable world.

4. **Harnessing Technology and Innovation:** The future of distance and online learning will be shaped by advancements in technology, pedagogy, and learning analytics. Emerging technologies such as artificial intelligence, virtual reality, and blockchain will continue to revolutionize online learning experiences, offering personalized, immersive, and data-driven educational experiences. Innovative pedagogical approaches, such as experiential learning, gamification, and microlearning, will enhance engagement and promote deeper learning outcomes.

5. **Commitment to Equity and Inclusion:** As we embrace the future of online learning, it is essential to remain steadfast in our commitment to equity, inclusion, and social responsibility. Efforts must be made to address digital divides, ensure accessibility for learners with diverse needs, and promote diversity and representation in online education. By prioritizing equity and inclusion, we can create learning environments that are accessible, welcoming, and empowering for all learners.

In conclusion, the future of distance and online learning holds immense potential for transforming education and empowering individuals and communities worldwide. By embracing technology, fostering innovation, and championing equity and inclusion, we can create a future where online education serves as a catalyst for individual growth, societal development, and global innovation. As we navigate the opportunities and challenges ahead, let us remain committed to the principles of excellence, equity, and social responsibility in advancing the field of online education. Together, we can build a brighter future where learning knows no boundaries.